Flower Fairies

POEMS AND PICTURES BY

CICELY MARY BARKER

LONDON PRIDE

BLACKIE: LONDON AND GLASGOW

WHERE?

Where are the fairies?
  Where can we find them?
We've seen the fairy-rings
  They leave behind them!

When they have danced all night,
  Where do they go?
Lark, in the sky above,
  Say, do you know?

Is it a secret
  No one is telling?
*Why, in your garden
  Surely they're dwelling!*

*No need for journeying,
  Seeking afar:
Where there are flowers,
  There fairies are!*

Blackie & Son Ltd., 5 Fitzhardinge Street, London, W.1
Bishopbriggs, Glasgow

Printed in Great Britain by Smith and Ritchie Ltd., Edinburgh

CONTENTS

WINTER ACONITE

Deep in the earth
I woke, I stirred.
I said: " Was that the Spring I heard?
For something called!"
" No, no," they said;
" Go back to sleep, go back to bed.

" You're far too soon;
The world's too cold
For you, so small."   So I was told.
But how could I
Go back to sleep?
I could not wait; I had to peep!

Up, up, I climbed,
And here am I.
How wide the earth! How great the sky!
O wintry world,
See me, awake!
Spring calls, and comes; 'tis no mistake.

Winter Aconite

CROCUS

Crocus of yellow, new and gay;
Mauve and purple, in brave array;
      Crocus white
      Like a cup of light,—
Hundreds of them are smiling up,
Each with a flame in its shining cup,
By the touch of the warm and welcome sun
Opened suddenly. Spring's begun!
Dance then, fairies, for joy, and sing
The song of the coming again of Spring.

Crocus

SCILLA

" *Scilla, Scilla, tell me true,*
Why are you so very blue?"

Oh, I really cannot say
Why I'm made this lovely way!

I might know, if I were wise.
Yet—I've heard of seas and skies,

Where the blue is deeper far
Than our skies of Springtime are.

P'r'aps I'm here to let you see
What that Summer blue will be.

When you see it, think of me!

Scilla

POLYANTHUS AND GRAPE
HYACINTH

" How do you do, Grape Hyacinth?
     How do you do?"
" Pleased to see *you*, Polyanthus,
     Pleased to see *you*,
With your stalk so straight and all your
    colours so gay."
" Thank you, neighbour! I've heard good
    news today."

" What is the news, Polyanthus?
     What have you heard?"
" News of the joy of Spring,
     In the song of a bird!"
" Yes, Polyanthus, yes, I heard it too;
That's why I'm here, with my bells in spires
    of blue."

Polyanthus and Grape Hyacinth

PERIWINKLE

In shady shrubby places,
Right early in the year,
I lift my flowers' faces—
O come and find them here!
My stems are thin and straying,
With leaves of glossy sheen,
The bare brown earth arraying,
For they are ever-green.
No great renown have I.   Yet who
Does not love Periwinkle's blue?

(Some Periwinkles are more purple than these; and every now and then you may find white ones.)

Periwinkle

NARCISSUS

Brown bulbs were buried deep;
Now, from the kind old earth,
Out of the winter's sleep,
    Comes a new birth!

Flowers on stems that sway;
Flowers of snowy white;
Flowers as sweet as day,
    After the night.

So does Narcissus bring
Tidings most glad and plain:
" Winter's gone; here is Spring—
    Easter again!"

Narcissus

FORGET-ME-NOT

Where do fairy babies lie
Till they're old enough to fly?
Here's a likely place, I think,
'Mid these flowers, blue and pink,
(Pink for girls and blue for boys:
Pretty things for babies' toys!)
Let us peep now, gently. Why,
Fairy baby, here you lie!

Kicking there, with no one by,
Baby dear, how good you lie!
All alone, but O, you're not—
You could *never* be—forgot!
O how glad I am I've found you,
With Forget-me-nots around you,
Blue, the colour of the sky!
Fairy baby, Hushaby!

Forget-me-Not

TULIP

Our stalks are very straight and tall,
 Our colours clear and bright;
Too many-hued to name them all—
 Red, yellow, pink, or white.

And some are splashed, and some, maybe,
 As dark as any plum.
From tulip-fields across the sea
 To England did we come.

We were a peaceful contry's pride,
 And Holland is its name.
Now in your gardens we abide—
 And aren't you glad we came?

(But long, long ago, tulips were brought from Persian gardens,
before there were any in Holland.)

Tulip

CORNFLOWER

'Mid scarlet of poppies and gold of the corn,
In wide-spreading fields were the Cornflowers
    born;
But now I look round me, and what do I see?
That lilies and roses are neighbours to me!
There's a beautiful lawn, there are borders
    and beds,
Where all kinds of flowers raise delicate heads;
For this is a garden, and here, a Boy Blue,
I live and am merry the whole summer
    through.
My blue is the blue that I always have worn,
And still I remember the poppies and corn.

Cornflower

ROSE

Best and dearest flower that grows,
Perfect both to see and smell;
Words can never, never tell
Half the beauty of a Rose—
Buds that open to disclose
Fold on fold of purest white,
Lovely pink, or red that glows
Deep, sweet-scented. What delight
  To be Fairy of the Rose!

Rose

PINK

Early in the mornings, when children still
    are sleeping,
Or late, late at night-time, beneath the
    summer moon,
What are they doing, the busy fairy people?
Could you creep to spy them, in silent magic
    shoon,

You might learn a secret, among the garden
    borders,
Something never guessed at, that no one
    knows or thinks:
Snip, snip, snip, go busy fairy scissors,
Pinking out the edges of the petals of the Pinks!

Pink Pinks, white Pinks, double Pinks, and
    single,—
Look at them and see if it's not the truth I tell!
Why call them Pinks if they weren't pinked
    out by *someone*?
And what but fairy scissors could pink them
    out so well?

Pink

GERANIUM

Red, red, vermilion red,
With buds and blooms in a glorious head!
There isn't a flower, the wide world through,
That glows with a brighter scarlet hue.
Her name—Geranium—ev'ryone knows;
She's just as happy wherever she grows,
   In an earthen pot or a garden bed—
    Red, red, vermilion red!

Geranium

CANTERBURY BELL

Bells that ring from ancient towers—
    Canterbury Bells—
Give their name to summer flowers—
    Canterbury Bells!
Do the flower-fairies, playing,
Know what those great bells are saying?
    Fairy, in your purple hat,
    Little fairy, tell us that!

" Naughty I know of bells in towers—
    Canterbury Bells!
Mine are pink or purple flowers—
    Canterbury Bells!
When I set them all a-swaying,
Something, too, my bells are saying;
Can't you hear them—*ding-dong-ding*—
    Calling fairy-folk to sing?"

Canterbury Bell

SHIRLEY POPPY

We were all of us scarlet, and counted as
    weeds,
  When we grew in the fields with the corn;
Now, fall from your pepper-pots, wee little
    seeds,
  And lovelier things shall be born!

You shall sleep in the soil, and awaken next
    year;
  Your buds shall burst open; behold!
Soft-tinted and silken, shall petals appear,
  And then into Poppies unfold—

Like daintiest ladies, who dance and are gay,
  All frilly and pretty to see!
So I shake out the ripe little seeds, and I say:
  " Go, sleep, and awaken like me!"

(A clergyman, who was also a clever gardener, made these
many-coloured poppies out of the wild ones, and named them
after the village where he was the Vicar.)

Shirley Poppy

CANDYTUFT

Why am I " Candytuft " ?
That I don't know!
Maybe the fairies
First called me so;
Maybe the children,
Just for a joke;
(I'm in the gardens
Of most little folk).

Look at my clusters!
See how they grow:
Some pink or purple,
Some white as snow;
Petals uneven,
Big ones and small;
Not very tufty—
No candy at all!

Candytuft

PHLOX

August in the garden!
Now the cheerful Phlox
Makes one think of country-girls
Fresh in summer frocks.

There you see magenta,
Here is lovely white,
Mauve, and pink, and cherry-red—
Such a pleasant sight!

Smiling little fairy
Climbing up the stem,
Tell us which is prettiest?
She says, "All of them!"

Phlox

SNAPDRAGON

Into the Dragon's mouth he goes;
    Never afraid is he!
There's honey within for him, he knows,
    Clever old Bumble Bee!
The mouth snaps tight; he is lost to sight—
    How will he ever get out?
He's doing it backwards—nimbly too,
    Though he is somewhat stout!

Off to another mouth he goes;
    Never a rest has he;
He must fill his honey-bag full, he knows—
    Busy old Bumble Bee!
And Snapdragon's name is only a game—
    It isn't as fierce as it sounds;
The Snapdragon Elf is pleased as Punch
    When Bumble comes on his rounds!

Snapdragon

LAVENDER

"*Lavender's blue, diddle diddle*"—
    So goes the song;
All round her bush, diddle diddle,
    Butterflies throng;
(They love her well, diddle diddle,
    So do the bees;)
While she herself, diddle diddle,
    Sways in the breeze!

"*Lavender's blue, diddle diddle,*
    Lavender's green";
She'll scent the clothes, diddle diddle,
    Put away clean—
Clean from the wash, diddle diddle,
    Hanky and sheet;
Lavender's spikes, diddle diddle,
    Make them all sweet!

(The word "blue" was often used in old days where we should say "purple" or "mauve".)

Lavender

GAILLARDIA

There once was a child in a garden,
  Who loved all my colours of flame,
The crimson and scarlet and yellow—
    But what was my name?

For " Gaillardia " 's hard to remember!
  She looked at my yellow and red,
And thought of the gold and the glory
    When the sun goes to bed;

And she troubled no more to remember,
  But gave me a splendid new name;
She spoke of my flowers as " Sunsets "—
    Then *you* do the same!

Gaillardia

SWEET PEA

Here Sweet Peas are climbing;
　(Here's the Sweet Pea rhyme!)
Here are little tendrils,
　Helping them to climb.

Here are sweetest colours;
　Fragrance very sweet;
Here are silky pods of peas,
　Not for us to eat!

Here's a fairy sister,
　Trying on with care
Such a grand new bonnet
　For the baby there.

Does it suit you, Baby?
　Yes, I really think
Nothing's more becoming
　Than this pretty pink!

Sweet Pea

HELIOTROPE

Heliotrope's my name; and why
People call me " Cherry Pie ",
That I really do not know;
But perhaps they call me so,
'Cause I give them such a treat,
Just like something nice to eat.
For my scent—O come and smell it!
How can words describe or tell it?
And my buds and flowers, see,
Soft and rich and velvety—
Deepest purple first, that fades
To the palest lilac shades.
Well-beloved, I know, am I—
Heliotrope, or Cherry Pie!

Heliotrope

MARIGOLD

Great Sun above me in the sky,
So golden, glorious, and high,
My petals, see, are golden too;
They shine, but cannot shine like you.

I scatter many seeds around;
And where they fall upon the ground,
More Marigolds will spring, more flowers
To open wide in sunny hours.

It is because I love you so,
I turn to watch you as you go;
Without your light, no joy could be.
Look down, great Sun, and shine on me!

Marigold

MICHAELMAS DAISY

" Red Admiral, Red Admiral, I'm glad to see
you here,
    Alighting on my daisies one by one!
I hope you like their flavour? and although
the Autumn's near,
    Are happy as you sit there in the sun?"

" I thank you very kindly, sir! Your daisies
are so nice,
    So pretty and so plentiful are they;
The flavour of their honey, sir, it really does
entice;
    I'd like to bring my brothers, if I may!"

" Friend butterfly, friend butterfly, go fetch
them one and all!
    I'm waiting here to welcome every guest;
And tell them it is Michaelmas, and soon the
leaves will fall,
    But *I* think Autumn sunshine is the best!"

Michaelmas Daisy

WINTER JASMINE

All through the Summer my leaves were
    green,
But never a flower of mine was seen;
Now Summer is gone, that was so gay,
And my little green leaves are shed away.
        In the grey of the year
        What cheer, what cheer?

The Winter is come, the cold winds blow;
I shall feel the frost and the drifting snow;
But the sun can shine in December too,
And this is the time of my gift to you.
        See here, see here,
        My flowers appear!

The swallows have flown beyond the sea,
But friendly Robin, he stays with me;
And little Tom-Tit, so busy and small,
Hops where the Jasmine is thick on the wall;
        And we say: " Good cheer!
        We're here! We're here!"

Winter Jasmine

To
ANNE
ELIZABETH
CAROLINE
KATHERINE
WATSON
*because they helped
to make this book*